Water Lilies

Instagram: @jacq.ann
Facebook:@waterliliesbyjacquelineann

Water Lilies

Jacqueline Ann

To order additional copies of this book, contact:
Xlibris
1-888-795-4274
www.Xlibris.com
Orders@Xlibris.com
753890

CONTENTS

Illustrated by Sean Anglim

for the bravery that it takes to be vulnerable.

like water lilies
we shall grace ourselves into the trust of liquid love
with life gently feeding our bellies one day at a time;
moments we cannot take in at once
people we cannot forget
choices that change us forever—
wetting the dryness of our innocence
pushing us to stand tall on the next sturdy leaf
we boldly prop ourselves on
to gain balance and fine composure
that somehow appears esteemed in the world;
we do this as if our hobbled minds don't
break down in private to pray that rocks lose their way
when skimming the surface of our souls in silence;
we want more, but we dread the leap—
we want change, but we reside comfortably
upon a single leaf—
we want air within our lungs that drives us deep,
but we choose to stare down
toward our buckling knees;
why are we afraid to be faithfully weak—
when the marks on our stretched legs
upon all our life leaps
birth us courage to create
and bravery to defeat?

Water Lilies is a collection of poetry
representative of a decade in time
that comprises a multitude of themes—
from love to loss, passion to pain,
suffering to healing, and life as a whole,
this poetry is inspired by the occurrences of loved ones and of oneself;
bound into book, these words within will solicit readers
to be courageous in their understanding of the poet's journey.
Offering an authenticity to the world around us,
Water Lilies chooses to showcase the beauty of truth in its natural state
and the necessity of undergoing distinctive emotions
in order to appreciate the gift of life
and to recognize each moment in life as a gift itself.

I

boy, did he have a smile that dripped and stained her mind
like a fine cabernet on white linen;
despite the times she tried to fight it,
the residue left was always just enough to remind her
of how hard it was
to wash him away.

—memories

you wish your eyes away
from dusk to dawn
placing them so gently into the pleasure of rest
on the assumption
that that is what they need;
and i love that about you—
you trust yourself to dream.

sometimes there are no words to express the gratitude you feel
when you hold a healer in your hands
but that was the thing about him—
he made me see what was wrong in this world
and i know that doesn't sound like something quite romantic
but to me, it was—
just whispering his name softly was like rescinding every past apology
i've ever professed for laughing nervously
wiping hidden tears that dripped down during the credits of a poignant movie
chocolate-boxing my truths,
suppressing a vulnerability that stirred up in my most heated moments;
these were some things in life
the wrong people i knew
once unknowingly asked me to conceal,
as if letting my heart beat unapologetically with freedom did not constitute
the greatest love story in itself.

—i love you

true love forgets
what the world wants
and remembers
what the soul needs.

i don't know many people who could get me to board a wooden coaster,
breathe deep to face a fear that has built over the years—
i don't know many people that could convince me that
dreary clouds in ashy skies create perfect days
to splash around a waterpark—
i don't know many people that made me care about the history
of a music band and what trials they've endured to embrace their success—
i don't know many people that prompt me to write
when i've had the longest day at work.

but then there's you.
and you make it all happen because i look at you
and i feel challenged
in the most honest way—
i feel challenged to want to live this life without fear
or negativity and beam a smile so large, so pure
that it traps those in its path,
commanding courage for all in choosing to see
the beauty and purpose woven into each day.

—but then there's you

i hope you find someone that makes it incredibly difficult every morning to leave your bed and go to work
someone who says "My treat!" and buys you dinner without expecting anything in return
someone that makes it exciting to buy them gifts and surprise them with all their favorites
someone that asks you to stop walking and gaze up at twinkling stars with them
someone who refuses to let go of your hand when the plane takes off
someone who is repulsed by the idea of teasing you about your insecurities
someone who tells you that you legitimately give them butterflies
someone who runs to the drugstore and buys everything you need when you fall ill
someone who starts a diet with you and works out with you so you're both on the same page
someone who encourages you to do something nice for a family member or a friend
someone who advises you to apologize first when you hurt someone
someone who picks you up when you're out with your friends and you've had too much to drink
someone that is equally excited to watch you achieve your goals and live your dreams
someone that blasts the music on the car ride and tells you to start dancing
someone that knows your day was rough, and while theirs wasn't much better, they calm themselves first before they calm you
someone who gives you the last piece of food on their plate
someone who rubs your back after a long day
someone who is kind to the waiter
someone who holds doors for strangers
someone who despises belittling other people
someone that cradles your face and kisses you hard with a certain passion you didn't even know existed

someone who is impressed with who you are and tells their friends and family all about you

someone who cares for you enough to swallow their pride to avoid unnecessary fights

someone whose face comforts yours when you spot it across the room at a loud party

someone who looks at you and sees every bit of beauty your parents saw since day one and then some

someone that sees your presence in their life as a gift and not just mere luck

someone that craves to be with you or just make you laugh when you're not even around

oh, i hope you find someone that destroys the rules to every love game ever played

someone that makes you laugh at the thought of wanting to stay single

truly

i just hope you find someone that happily takes their shoes off when they walk into your life

for once they feel the warmth of your heart

they will know you as their new home and will want to stay forever

i hope you find that someone.

i don't believe people
when they tell me they are incapable of being in love
we fall in love every day
with circadian miracles—the way the sun hits our hair
the tears that stroll leisurely down our cheeks in laughter
the cultures of people we cross
it doesn't matter where quite honestly
a city draped in palms, a city dazzled in lights
a suburban home, fenced and grassed with scheduled movie nights.
a winter, genial sun that brush upon lost deer
or sand that sink our toes inshore as waves wash off our fear.
canals streaming rivers of love, oh, so soft and sweet
and roman fountains carved in stone with coins for those that seek.
grapevines to crawl upon terra-cotta tiles afar
or Tuscan hills rolled in greenery that heal all pains of the heart.
it doesn't matter where quite honestly
when love is there to write the scene;
the wind to your hair
the water in your skin
the beams from your eyes
oh, but love is just in everything.

my hands were far quicker than his mostly because
i stole it like free bathroom amenities
before an eleven a.m. checkout at some high-rise, lavish hotel;
someone needed to show him that i meant business
for a bogus reach could never be me;
and such the courteous battle over candlelight ceased
as he surrendered a thank you and uttered softly
"one day, you know what will be nice?
when it doesn't matter who wins,
because it comes from one account."

—date night

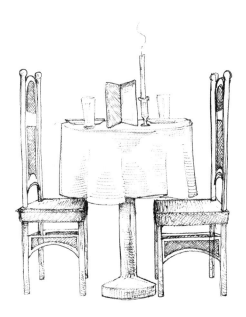

we never quite capture the defining moments or clear memories
that help us leap from young to old
smooth to wrinkled
waxed up to worn out
when we are too busy laughing through them
and running through them
protecting loved ones through them
oh, how we cry through them
and hurt through them
it is relative to us
and unrelated all at once;
how the tiny pains and pleasures
we ask to pass and pause
are braided in blocks of time
we scream at
"slow down!"

—time flies

"i'm still here"

"why did you stay?"

it floated out of his mouth like a breeze
that was blessed to blast away
any reason i ever flung back into his face to leave me;
it all went away, so far away in just a few simple words of his—

"i'm here because i want to be here,"

brushing a strand of my hair back
that adhered to my upper lip,
it was him to speak again,

"and i want to be here, forever."

she's the kind of girl that waited her whole life to roll
onto the other side of the bed
at the crack of dawn and gaze with passionate smiles
at the one man that proved them all wrong—
the one that made his way into her heart
without her ever feeling like her heart should be open
for her to feel loved;
the one who discerned each individual ingredient
God had ever so gently stirred inside her soul
as he chose all his nights to lay his head, still,
upon a pillow next to hers—

for the love he had shown in his commitment,
and boy, was he committed to loving her.

even the ocean was jealous of his eyes—
the abundance of life that swam toward his coast
emanating throughout the night
refracting light rays on the breaks of his waves
falling forward,
falling back,
with each whisper to her ear;
and how the depths of him measured miles for days
fathoms down below
distant shores disappeared
a humming
a rhythm
a chant she vaguely heard
"oh, infinite levels of charcoaled trenches
and sulfurous currents
dry her fears, whet her mind, and bring her soul back to the surface!"
what was it about him?
she looked around searching frantically
an anchor
a life jacket
an oxygen tank
a reason
a passing whim
and collecting them confidently
they became strong enough to uphold her convictions
for why she should not swim
what was it about him?
and yet her complexion crumbled
clenching fists, closing eyes, shaking knees
hastened thoughts, mumbled words, breathing deep
a new choice, submit
her beautiful self over board
to a world unknown
she was swallowed up
lost at sea with the stars
treading with laughter, quakes of passion rumbled through her bones

drowning her fear of being submersed by some cold, vicious undertow;
but that's when she knew
to seek a boundless love
one mustn't be afraid to be weak
for we will never be found
if we're never lost
if we are never lost at sea.

somewhere inside the universe
stretched beyond our glorious galaxy
that night lay the story
of you and i.
looming low above us
a calm and placid crescent
penetrating pieces of its silver love
into the bunkers of your well rested eyes
trickling down
like a triple chocolate fountain
to the glass tips of your tender tongue
we tasted all our hesitations
and yet
we dropped to our knees with cackles so loud
that even the stars blushed bashfully—
for that was the night
it became astronomically known
that the universe had found harmony.

—the first kiss

so when the fight was over
i learned that my angel had stronger muscles than his demon.

i suppose now that is exactly why the growth in rejection hurts;
someone must be willing to take the punches in between
and when God saw resilience parading in my heart
proudly,
He chose me.

—listen

i don't want to kiss who they think you are.
i want to kiss who you want to become.
i want you
every bit of you—
your windows
your cracks
your lights.
i see you
every bit of you—
your sunsets
your dreams
your nights.

your parents smile across the living room because they know
as we stand in this kitchen corner
on the dawn of a Saturday,
arguing which plates are not clean on the countertop
twenty-something years ago,
so did they.

—the beginnings in love

after all
a girl can be told she's beautiful her whole life,
but she may never believe it
until she meets a man
whose eyes can speak it
louder than his lips.

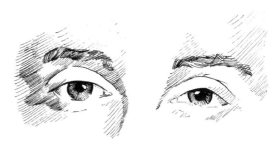

he buried his face into her chest
kissing all the tender parts on her skin
and only her hands could respond
with a simple clasp to his head
changing complexities in her breath
she reached up soliciting to find
any oxygen wavering above her head
that was still there to remind her
of the necessity to breathe in such moments
when his hands were made to make
her forget.

baby, don't make me promises
with that tongue of yours
when i know that your hands
have learned to speak
a different language.

he felt her
like a palm cupping in gratitude
grains of blissful sand
falling off salted fingers
proudly exhaling the memory of enduring
a stark and brisk winter; oh, but
he chose her—
like how fish chose to breathe in the sea
and the sun chose to dance with the moon
as a loving guide when she sleeps;
he loved her so
just as that quilted blanket entrusted to brush his
bare back and halt his youthful mind
from drifting off to dark dreams as a boy;
but as a man, he drifted toward a substance
circulating inside her veins;
and whatever it was,
he knew her well—
well enough to know his lips from that moment on
could never be used in pursuit to speak
another woman's name.

i'm proper
until you touch me
i control
until you disarm me
i want nothing
until you want me.
this part of you
that makes me lose
and win
in the blink of an eye;
you had to have this part of you within
that makes this love run in circles
we chase throughout the night.

the mistake we make when we want to fall in love
is not understanding the fullness of our lover's spirit—
when the spirit soars much like a firecracker
it's only natural for us to hold them
marvel at their beauty in our palms
and out of love, we do this;
but as we stifle their soar up to the skies
and who is to say that
we cannot get burned?
it's never freedom that a spirit craves
for a spirit that is wise knows they are already free
but we fear them leaving
and changing
and needing others more than they need us
holding them so tightly
to us, it is love
but love is greater than we know it to be
love hits the sky
with one thousand polychromic streams
and it is flawless—
love sends the sparks in one another to
extraordinary levels and illuminates a darkness
found in many;
you see, as we love
we hold until it hurts
but as we fall in love
it is more gratifying to watch that spirit soar
knowing that their purpose is different than ours
and trusting that what is true to come home will always come home
and what was meant to live will never die.

love knocked loudly
as walls fell down
and you were the ears i wanted
to hear such a sound.

—thank you

casual car rides
playful rain, and coffee Sundays filled
the memoirs in the minds of our twenties
do you remember the day
my heart took a leap
in the front seat?

"i've never met anyone like you,"

rumbling through the doors inside his car
it came from a place within my heart i hadn't accessed in years;
and with ample gallantry, he located that place within himself too
driving out all my reason for anchoring such fear,
his words released recollections
i once harbored for history and tears—

"i felt i hadn't met myself either,
until i met you."

i never knew passion was a suffering
until i watched myself grow anxiously in love
with all the things that push my heart around
and pin it up against a wall
bullying it
to watch it
love itself so much—
bullying it
to watch it just want
everything and anything in this world
all at once.

falling in love
is the fourth-grade teacher who told you to go home that night
and write an essay about anything you want
struggling with writer's block
and marveling at the notion of a free assignment
you've found yourself stuck
because for the first time
it scares you
to hold a pen with
the power and possibility
of choosing to create something out of nothing.

he rode on every back road to her heart
winding trails she did not see
streets she forgot to block off
with cones of caution
and broken memories
he stopped at every town corner
to learn all of her shop names
knowing those who take love's highway
drive too fast
to ever stay.

and if we're being honest
i never saw you coming.
i never saw us walking down nature trails,
coasting off to a beach somewhere,
hysterically laughing and dancing in my bedroom with no music,
wrapping presents for our families, painting on easels,
blissfully trailing ourselves through the city snow
in silent laughter—
but in the morning,
i fell in love with you slowly.
i suppose i never needed the sun to rise and
pour itself onto your silken skin through window cracks
for me to see that you retain a light
that awakens me.

i want to cross all of your bridges
i want to know all of your lands
and every wave that breaks
oceans within you
i want to want
all that i can.

your love paints me in hues
even the spectrums on a color wheel
are jealous of.

you don't know
the sensation that pulses an aftershock
quaking through my body when you move
one inch toward my frame;
you don't know
how i've captured your scent
and held it hostage in the cells of my skin
forcing them to revisit me
as your headlights peer off my driveway;
you don't know how the prickled edges of your face
tickle my lips and how i feel your grin bulging
as the corners of our mouths make love;
you knew nothing of this
but how can you
when i tripped into this trap of
neglect and forgot
our love is customized?
our love is anything but ordinary,
and you deserve to hear words
no one has ever spoken before;
you deserve to read more sentences that cry,
"i love you,"
damn it—
you deserve
to be loved more.

there were several times throughout the night i found to be strange
at a loud noisy bar, just us
standing in the corner with our drinks
in the car ride back, just us
holding hands and no radio
to a public eye, it's easy to stipulate
our minds were elsewhere, disconnected
and with honesty, if i watched myself that night from a distance
i may have assumed the same—
and yet i used to think every moment needed to be filled
filled with laughter or conversation
that would grant us one step closer to understanding
who we were and how we came to be.
but i never found success with someone by filling every moment
for i never really let the moments settle themselves
the sighs sink in, the eye contact lingers
the bashful smirks inch slowly
and yet how beautiful is it
for two human beings to find quiet
and still feel tied?
how beautiful is it
for two human beings to silence their mouths
so that their souls can speak?

the sun was getting sleepy
but i stayed awake so that
i could feel what it would be like
to love you
in the dark.

i am glad you cannot understand how much i love you.
i am glad it is such an incomprehensible amount that
words of our language are incapable to satisfy with speech;
and darling,
i am glad you cannot see what we hold in our infinity—
for we live in a world where the sight in our eyes knows limit,
but love,
the love we breathe
should not.

i didn't know what it was
until i was thirty-six thousand feet above the Atlantic
watching these tears roll off
the left wing and
drop
into an oceanic infinity
that also understood the depth
of what great courage
your love had given me.

—i knew i loved you then

the sea and the stars—
they knew about us
long before we did.

falling in love
is blissfully dancing as i write up
the world's largest run-on sentence
and never quite caring if all the English teachers in my past
met together for coffee with pile of red pens
and a boatload of scrutiny
as they mark up the heart of honesty
i poured out onto this page.

—truth be told

i lay in our bed and i kiss you goodnight
you've fallen asleep, for your eyes lost the fight
but to me that is fine, for i love to see you dream
your vulnerability breeds such beauty when you're next to me;
i lay in our bed and i feel no more pain
when i dream of the day we'll be three with your name
and maybe he will find the woman of his dreams
like how his father had courage to come and find me;
or maybe she will fight for true love until the end,
trusting God to protect her heart and bring her a good man;
i lay in our bed and i pray for it all—
i know it works now, but life throws curve balls;
so when glass breaks and tears that form are real,
it will only be God that our hearts do seek to hold and to heal;
i lay in our bed and i know we will age,
but we will never feel old if we choose
to laugh the whole way.

love—
in all forms, defines the universe of which we exist;
whether there be a lack of it
or an overabundance—
all things created have been created
to be measured and understood
through a single unit of love.

love will make you do crazy things
even if you were never that girl who didn't care
if the boy who just paid for your dinner
actually got home safe
or you were too busy to wonder if he thought of you that day—
you will be reversed
you will be tested
you will be humiliated in the most beautiful way
that's what love does.
it challenges our comforts to expand beyond ourselves
and it makes us say silly things that we wouldn't care to say to other people
it makes us angry, tough, and want to start over leading life by ourselves
without the assistance of someone else
and needing their love to make us smile daily;
but in the end
we don't leave
we can't
because with one smile, one apology, one look in the eye
we know innately we have a heart that was greatly designed
to pump blood for two souls, not one.
and maybe it's humbling inside to admit that we found someone, for once,
that's worth that extra pump.

it wasn't his romantic profession that frightened me
it was my heart that beat louder when words left his mouth
it wasn't fear that watered my eyes
it was his genuine delivery that made me feel chosen
pointing to his lips, he said his words were only words,
and it would never be enough to show me the great in his love,

"i don't want you to hear it. i need you to feel it."

tugging my hands and placing them on his beating chest
to outline and abridge a pulsing life of truth within him
oh, as whispers crawled from underneath his breath,

"do you feel that?"
"do you feel that?"

and i choked up—
for how could i not release a tear in a moment like this
at the sight of a man choosing a life of vulnerability
and a man who chose it
for me.

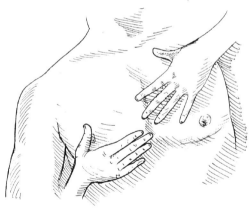

our lips do not just stop it
they bend it
seamlessly, back and forth
bouncing in between tenses of our lives
and whether he knew this or not—
his touch whispers goodbye and wipes the past stains of ex-lovers
my hands feel him hello as they know what we can build
our eyes laugh playfully
as they peel back layers to unleash and define
the moments we make in present time
to strengthen the core of who we are
and who we are choosing to become—
oh, but every so often we share this kiss
long enough to dim
the now of this world
strong enough to visit
his past, my past
his future, my future
respectfully—
laying roses on graves for personal failures and losses we had to endure
glorifying gains by giving praise of how hard we chose to work
dreaming a duet of what successes we will hold
desiring to be the one the other calls home
because every so often we share this kiss
and it startles the dimensions of time.

—that kind of kiss

and like a great novel
i would have read you for years
chuckling with your comics
piecing all your pains
and toasting all your triumphs
humbly acclaimed—
keeping you bound to my chest
for never shall you rest
upon some dusted old shelf that dulls
the glory of your name.

he tickled her in bed
shouting that he had
no money to give
and she laughed so loud
as if the thought of running at that very moment
was just as repulsive as only staying
if he had shouted the contrary
but she was wise to walk a speed—
slow enough that let her observe
the life choices that pressed themselves onto his worn hands
careful callouses layered over
a palm of honesty that explained
the safe and strong
silent and soulful
passionate heart
to beat under his deep chest
and then she saw it—
there were going to be things in this world
some of the wealthiest men
will never be able to buy
and it would be him to offer her
the unsellable.

for her, it was always the dawn;
how the world never asked if she was awake
there she lie
playfully on the cushions of this planet
praying and praising the glory of silence—
her hair swept in beautiful locks
of care and carelessness alone and
perfumed in a bouquet of dawn grass
as her ears phished out murmurs in trees
jingling leaves
and gusts of wind in the distance
she arched her back to brush the dew drops that kissed her soul tenderly,
beaming stars in her eyes
and love in her lips—
she was alive
she was happy
she was healthy
she was in love.

you asked me if i would ever write something for you
and without hesitation, i proclaimed no—
what a puzzled look grew calmly on your face
like you questioned if i enjoyed your company
as much as you enjoyed mine
but reality speaks more than i can—
my words weren't just art for the world to reckon with
they are my heart, my beats, my open wounds, my insecurities
my faith, my love, my gentle, my rough, my shield, and my sword;
yet slowly, my words became a co-pay
to grant myself residency on a lovely sofa for one hour
facing a silent soul, a brownish clipboard, and a moving pen—
i never wanted you to be a part of that world
you are my peace, not my escape
and for that, you always will be;
centuries will pass, and if someone ever finds the novel i hold buried to tell our
story
if someone ever fans through it with waves of curiosity
i pray there are no creases marked
no coffee stains dripped, no tears, no cutouts, no pulls
i pray every single page is drawn blank
for in the life we lived together
i need to know that i told you everything you meant to me
and the moments we shared became memories sacred only to us—
ones the world could not relive in print, creating some frenzied debate
for high school students on a Wednesday during literature class to determine
what kind of pulsing and passionate, brave love we once shared—

i need to know that time never paused, casting doubts upon us
and striking through lines of our life with ink
i need to know how your love was always particular
having the hands of a healer to steal my pen and create a home
i never needed to run from
so no, i will never write you
because for the rest of my life
i will love you.

from the incision across her stomach that it took to get me out
to making sure i always had enough food and water
to the fact that i was always clean and dressed with dignity
to the first time i was ever brought to church and my religious beliefs were born
to all the fun memories before i started kindergarten
and how i learned to read and write before school ever started
to the time i cried at my pre-k graduation because i couldn't see her in the audience and she came up to get me
to all the school events she attended, and all the little arts and crafts she told me she loved
to her helping me lift up my broken left arm at three-years-old and exercise it post-surgery
to her packing my lunch and leaving me hidden post-it notes inside
to her knowing who my most recent crush was and purposely interacting with them just to see me smile
to all the birthday parties she planned for me
to the times there was a present on my bed when i got home from a long day at school with a note that read, "just because i love you"
to the time she followed my school bus on my first day so when i nervously looked out the window, i saw her
to the moment she taught me how to play the piano which changed my life
to the first serious talk about life and boys i ever had with her on the edge of my bed one late night
to making me burst out laughing at the most serious and inopportune moments
to the moment when i got in trouble in school and she had my back through it all
to her not tolerating how hurtful and immature kids were as i was growing up
she gave me a confidence unlike no other to stand up for myself and for others
to listening to my repeated stories, rambling on about people in my life and things that wouldn't matter in a year or so
to the times my heart was crushed and the tears wouldn't stop flowing and she picked up every piece of me, just by being there
to the random fights—wouldn't change a thing
to the long hugs, the tissues, the laughter, the goals to change for the better from it, the shopping excursions, the vows and the strength needed she gave me to power through tough times
to the words of wisdom that she gave me for what i needed to help others

to showing me that it is beautiful to love unconditionally
to give endlessly even to those who never say thank you or give back
to forgive even when you are beyond hurt
to be kind and to those who need it most
to pray for the souls that were forgotten
to be thankful for many blessings
to run to, not away, from God when your life feels lost
to showing me never to be too prideful to say "i am sorry" and "i was wrong"
to being honest and pointing things out to help others become better people—

For being this incredible human being and nurturing mother that has grown and become a woman I firmly admire and respect. When I was younger, my mind was constantly occupied by things that I can't even remember now. It's ok because it got me to where I am now. At twenty-one years old, I can say that I finally get it. I see the sacrifices made, the pains, the boundless love poured, the dreams and aspirations deferred, the never ending compassion, the weaknesses' of humanity, the strengths, and how one life can change so many. I see a person just like me who tries day after day to be better than who she was the day before. I see a person whose positivity is infectious and loves to see others smile. And I see a person who is loved by so many both in this life and in the next. My mother is a gift to me, my whole family, and more importantly to this world. She is a soul that God is proud of. I am so beyond thankful for my best friend, who I am privileged to call my mother.

—for my beautiful mother

when i dream of your smile
i do not dream of the crease
the formation
the beautiful dimple
or your perfect, shining teeth that crystalize behind your soft lips
for your physicality alone is not enough to define you.
i dream of what words make you feel safe
what jokes make you laugh
what touches make you crumble
and what moments make you sad.
when i dream of you
i do not dream of all your successes and biggest moments
for i find more love in watching you grow
struggle, and persevere to become the success that stands tall
on the days you alone made possible.
when i dream of you
i do not dream of my dreams
but of yours instead because they matter to me
just as much as they do for you—
in closing my eyes
i dream for you
and only you.
for when i dream of you
i dream not selfishly.

i used to think a relationship was something i had to prove
like i had to accomplish something
as the fear of my solidarity could be struck away with a simple choice of
seating myself on some roller coaster that propelled itself from zero to sixty
in one beat of my heart
the clicking of the bar auto locking pressed itself into my mind
along with the steel wedge that made it a point to keep me in place—
many people like this in relationships
not wondering if they will fall out at any minute
or trusting that there is security to guard them
and it's all part of the thrill
it's all part of the ride and the nerves
as we trail up tracks, slowly on a steep incline
anticipating a drop to come
a screaming to come
a gravitational pull to come
a confusion in our bellies to arise
where our brain signals overlap laughing, crying, and yelling,
and somehow, i was so focused on feeling all of that
believing that's what the world wanted me to feel—
locked in and filled with hysteria
that's how the world wanted me to date because that's how others dated—
but with him,
i never had to do that.
i didn't have to commit the most daunting, loftiest ride in the park
the one that gets written up in national newsletters,
in order to understand myself a little bit better.
a relationship didn't have to form from slinging sincerity onto a shelf,
feeling out of place and testing my fear and faith daily;
a relationship didn't have to be the feeling of waiting for a steep drop
and wondering if i can survive it;
this whole time maybe the relationship i was searching for was the
wrong one—
maybe the relationship i deserved was different than what i expected.
maybe the relationship that would last with me was not going
to be the one that spins
high, fast, low, slow, pacing, anxious, rushing,
griping, pushing, pulling, stopping, going in one ride;

maybe the relationship i would fall in love to know was
motionless—
still in time—
the breath of air we exhale after a ride is over,
a clammy hand that grasps another's as the roller coaster ascends uphill,
a calm blue sky we catch midsight as our heads whip around the corner;
maybe the reason why i love him is because he reminds me of
nothing i've known,
but something i should have—
he is the moment to exist between moments
for they are the most honest, simple, and kindest pieces of time
to experience that exhibit the human condition in its most
beauteous and permeable state—
and i cannot tell you
how lovingly hard
that is to find.

the days of my young—
i remember myself being
tossed up like a pop catch
towards a sky bright skylight
and in your arms i would fall;
the first man i learned to trust in this life
it was you—
you were it all.
thunder roars in the summer
and bad dreams that lurked in nights
you were the calm i knew i had
the calm i could always find—
many hats i wore then
mainly because of you
the way you believed in who i was
and all that i could do.
changing sports like changing clothes
next day i had all the gear
didn't matter if i had the talent
when your love never failed to hear
all that i desired
and the dreams that i chased
they changed from day to day
but still-
you kept my pace
and when did i become this woman
from soccer goalie to CPA
and all the good i've done
because you've encouraged confidence
to arise in me each day-
and for all the evenings we talked
on the back deck at home
you understood the root of my troubles
reminding me that i am never alone;
i've conquered so many feats in life as i traveled
because you were not afraid
to lighten the burden i carried
i see now the sacrifices that you made;

some mornings you are gone
before i even open my eyes
i admire the strength that it takes
to lead your kind of life-
and so i've dipped my toes
into a world somewhat like yours
and from that alone,
my heart has grown
to understand what true love endures.
oh, and the advice you've given me
i've used to help those in need
dad, i hope you know that because of you
i am more than i could ever dream.

—for my incredible father that i love so much

II

i wrote a best seller one night
in my dreams
but i woke to find that i was
only asleep
and to learn that dreams deferred are dreams
that die
when you are the only one
that keeps them
alive.

—chase the dream

it's time to make romance jealous;
it's time to find love around you
in this world one thousand ways
that are anything but
romantic.

i have missed the awakening of a three a.m.
not from dreams that haunt me,
but rather a simple plea of poetic dehydration,
an absolute thirst and waterslide of words,
that rush themselves down
toward the tips of my fingers
seeking shelter on the shells
of letter cases awaiting to be struck;
i have missed the awakening of a three a.m.
not from heartbreak or soulful revelation,
but rather from a simple plea of invigoration,
an absolute gust to carry this heart
and birth it to the world with trickles of truth
that triumph and tremor
from what it loves most—
an English ecstasy.

the first time i tried to write a poem,
i worried myself,
counting syllables and forcing rhymes
in the sixth grade.
because it was rare
to prompt poetic bravery that rips the training wheels off and
pedals the bike alone;
the teacher stood in front of the class,
and before our pens hit paper, she said,

"show me what you want to say
don't just tell me."

what a simple sentence to gift our youth,
knowing the greatest complexities of growing up in the years to come
would soon be knocking on our doors,
and somehow, remembering those words would become
the strongest way to open.

she laughed about how her first kiss was so awkward
as if it should have been something else
more certain
more commercial
more cinematic
to be worth a wide lens on a Canon
an iMax sold out to lonesome critics
sensitive boyfriends dragged to the seats
and salty popcorn flinging out of greased buckets
over pop cans
on opening night.

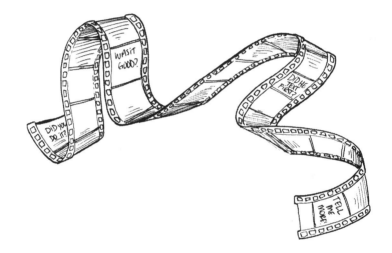

bravery does not always put on a uniform.
sometimes bravery puts on a white tee,
ripped jeans, and pulls back a bun full of wet hair—
staring into a mirror,
bravery reassures itself that there are other colors
that exist in this world worth beholding to its eyes
even if the only one its brain chooses to see
is gray.

—a light for those in the dark

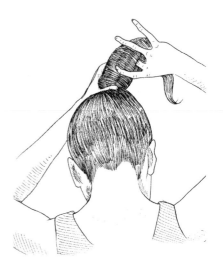

and there it was,
from woman to woman, i saw it;
in the doorway, it was happening—
as i listened to her romantic professions
only thirty years of life had separated us,
but even time has a way of never cutting what a woman craves;
time doesn't steal the sugar in our eyes that sparkles with relief,
when our hearts find reason again
to beat in rhythm with a rest for appreciation—
to be respected
to be loved
to be understood
to be wanted
to be needed
to be healed
to be protected
to not be taken lightly
but to be held and nurtured like a fledgling, shaking, preflight
despite the confidence in our wingspan
it is what we all want,
and it is what we will never say.
for it is the pain of the past
or fear of the future
that restrains us and cripples our faith in believing
that there is one other bird that wants to soar too
that there is one other bird that wants to know
when, how, and where to find us flying, free
in this limitless sky.

—fall in love at any age

absence makes the heart grow fonder
is that what they always say
as i feel myself scramble in ache to release you
into the light of a new day.

—moving on

and when it's time, i will tell him the truth;
the world will judge him harshly for how many women he can score,
how many hearts he can break,
how many weights he will lift,
how many dollars he will make,
how many tears he cannot shed,
how many mean jokes he should make,
how many punches he will throw,
how many dangerous things he will try,
how many friends he will keep,
how many enemies he will burn,
and how many times he should not look weak.
that's when i will look him in the eye
and tell him that the world around him will never know his heart
the way God does;
for the world will not be there for him when he falls,
and because of that alone,
it should never earn a place high enough in his mind
to dictate how he should live his life.
this world is scared of men with hearts that give away love so softly
and command respect from within—
for they are fearless,
they are brave,
and they are fighters for us all.
so when it is time to tell him
i will tell him the truth:
exploring the world through the perception of others
will only weather his skin,
but dressing himself in God's armor to fight
will make it tough for the world to touch him.

—a letter to my son

i do not know it for cozy-knit sweaters
crunchy, sweet apples sizzling in caramel sauce
or pots filled with pumpkin cream soup on simmer.
i cannot see it merely with candlelight flickering
on the frames of dark windowsills
or aromas dripping in cinnamon spice
to creep through the halls of a home.
i do not feel it when trees burst into flames
that burn and bust love to crisps
an expo in indefinite hues unlike no other.
i do not hear it when crowds roar for a fumble-intercept
and test-drive all decibels of sound on a television.
i cannot touch it with vast and tenebrous coal skies
that sparkle in glittered specks among the descent of a chilled night.
i do not know it for the things that come and go
and though i choose my love for it with all its temporal treasure,
i feel it most for the lesson it lends to mankind—
for even in nature's death
there is a beauty to remain
as it asserts that a finale is never final;
for there is only and just only
change.

—the lessons of autumn

66

so often i feel that writer's block is the enemy
yet many writers become acquainted
with such an insidious occlusion
the more they crack a smile
laugh the good laugh
and maybe even meet a soul worth loving;
suddenly, it feels like their ballpoint flames are not searing enough
to sauté tasty words
and to film some steamy passion
that the world could plop itself upon a couch
on a Friday night to press play
and deem it to be worthy—
yet, what about our worth?
is it not worth something to enjoy the fruits of a sustaining smirk
to replace three a.m.'s that we once devoured some pen in frustrated fury
tortured by scattered memories that refused to heal us?
isn't it worth something
to know there could be a time in this life
where we indulge ourselves in reading
a love story we didn't have to write,
but rather was written for us instead?

—now we're living

only a writer knows how to count seconds
precisely and perfectly
as we hold our breath
vulnerably
sending our soul out to sea
to be rescued
by our closest friends and family
patient for some response
that is more than obligation
but rather
a haven of gut-wrenching ecstasy
hang-on-the-fridge worthy
punch-the-air
type of replication—
as if their opinions are what drives us to do what we love
as if their opinions matter enough to revolutionize
the fire that already feeds us
the very millisecond
we make love to words.

why do we apologize on behalf of our family
when new people fall into the picture?
"we're not usually like this"
"they're so crazy, i'm sorry"
what is this madness that crawled into our veins
and changed the thickness of our blood
to make us feel like it should be as thin as water
so that our guests feel as if they can drink it too?
but they cannot
they are not us
and welcoming them is not to hide what we are
but to invite them in being a part of the craze.
so please don't stop
keep the cackles loud, and
drink the extra beer
tell the provocative jokes at dinner
blast the tunes that bring you back
cut the cake before you sing
hang the Christmas lights in the backyard on that one little tree
that came from your grandmothers' side of the family
write your own words to a jingle
laugh about the times you were a bad child
do it all because it means something—
and life is not long enough to strip our sincerity
in pacifying those who linger into our homes
with opinion.

we cracked a bottle of red
and cuddled each other on the corner of our couch
wondering when life pulled the rug out
under our sturdy feet
from porcelain dolls
to paying bills and
Flintstone vitamins
to placing pills
on the tips of our tongues
just so we could understand
this world
the same free way
we once did
as kids.

good parents
will raise a house
and build their children
on a foundation to intuitively find
north, south, east, and west
just by standing on their front porch.
and yet, latched on their coat pocket lies a compass—
not because good parents believe they will use it,
but because they recognize someone else on their children's journey will,
and not everyone has a parent with time to give direction;
for when getting lost in life is common,
it becomes harder to show others how to come home.

—change the world, starting at home

in life,
there are times that you don't know you are living
inside a small passing canvas
painting it with the colors of joy
until someone else shows you the warmth and the beauty
you just created in that
minute but momentous
piece of time.

III

i didn't want to perfume him day and night
with glamorous spritz of cold vanilla tobacco
or some crystal noir soaked in lush roses that clutched his scent for miles.
he would have loved it, i know that,
but i was not born to be a trail.
i was not born to be fragranced fog with a need to be worn,
and i was not born to greet lust and part with love.
i tried hard to fight that because i never wanted to wear off.
this fear of fading drowned me of how
i would not be remembered after one sweep of wind.
and though it be silly,
it holds much veracity that no woman wants to be forgotten
by a man that her heart has purely chosen.
so day in and day out,
i made a choice—to strike this scent, shake the glass,
and remain a caffeinated roast to travel up and bond
to the pores of his mind.
i let no time pass for me to become a precedence of truth
in clearing his palette;
and with all of this,
i had made it known by my audacity
that when he loses his way,
i no longer choose to be the reason why;
but now the reason why he came back to his senses.

the air obstructing strobes formed clouds of vanilla smoke
over their cautiously romantic and apprehensive minds—
puffs and puffs calmly vacillating,
between the giggles and glares,
beneath the smiles his heart was not beating for her,
she knew.
above it all, she would realize life could bring her more,
he knew.
but together under dreamy lights, they ascertained a desired comfort—
dancing with diplomacy in unison,
becoming wallflowers to their words,
and politely waiting for life to waltz in on lead,
whisk him left—
whisk her right.

i wouldn't mind falling in love
with someone on the other side of this world—
better to measure the distance in
miles than moments
i spent trying to find the heart in the man who first laid in my bed—
the one i made vows to,
and love to,
night after night
to only crash to my knees,
pleading him
to come back home.

i knew something was wrong
when my bedtime calling became me falling
asleep in the dark;
it was never me to choose
the indefinite and the unknown—
i entrusted myself to it:
a final comfort of where i was,
a place i could identify with,
a place that was quiet enough to hear tears stream
and that worried me—
for i never chose darkness over light,
but this night was different—
darkness chose me.

he didn't have to travel very far for her to feel his distance—
she tasted it every night in his kiss.

i think i changed the most when i realized
he celebrated seven less birthdays than you,
and yet
his lips spoke kinder, softer words.
his eyes have seen less of life,
and yet
he has seen more of me.
a quality so rare to comprehend—
i thought you lived long enough to have it too.
but my first mistake was fighting faith
on the notion that you were becoming a man
that was never meant to be you.

—older is not wiser

we couldn't place our faults on a map
and pinpoint the longitude and latitude of where it all went wrong.
but we knew one thing for sure;
our love lay in mud, and our lust danced in the rain;
how could we ever pursue such a paradoxical pain?
all chaos tapped itself to our once connected vein—
and drinking us softly,
we drifted away.

do you ever just stop
and let someone hug you tight
and listen to them when they say calm down
as you feel your thick pulse slow itself softly?
do you ever just laugh
and let someone tickle you hard
and scream at them with death threats
as you untangle yourself from their power pin, howling?
do you ever just scream
and let life talk its way into your head
and allow yourself to entertain pessimism in your weaknesses
as you search for one person on this earth that cares enough
to hear your loathing list and rebut each one?
do you ever just cry
and let suffering lay itself out
and hear your heart whimper on the inside
pleading for such a pain to pass over you?
i sometimes wonder.

—do you ever

heartache
is driving home betrayed
by the hopes of what you dreamed them to be
and feeling the skies open up
as you keep tapping the gas
noticing that it's no longer water
but rather blood
to be swooshing itself
contentedly around
your windshield glass
covering every square inch of vision
you need to keep moving forward
as your heartbeat slows
amused at your faintness
until all you can do is hazardously pull over
onto the side of the road
throw your face
into your palms, hysterical
and pray—
pray for it to stop.

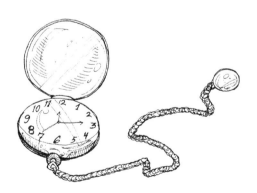

she was the space between his fingers for parting,
and the distance to his dreams from this earth;
she was the memory bin that held every birthday card,
and the top button on his favorite dress shirt;
he failed to see her presence
or who she was in all her simple worth,
but when she left,
he gasped for breath—
for was he lonely
or was he hurt?

he thought he won the game
when he let her go
got away with getting
and not having to give
but he didn't know
he picked up and played with
the most beautiful glow stick
his heart would ever find
and so he broke her
left and right
casual smirks inching on his face
that were quickly wiped
he grew fiercely afraid
unexpected and awake
grew her vibrant shine
it was then he met regret
for the first time
in his life.

we toggle on the crack beneath our feet
not quite sure why we cannot stand on the same side;
flirting,
we await a shift of danger—
so please tell me,
when the ground shakes
and what we built breaks,
whose fault will it be?

we bathed in silence because we loved more
that our bodies could speak
the *i'm sorry*s
we were too damn proud to say.

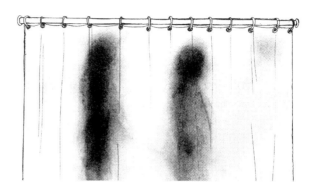

and on that dismal night,
i saw every blade of wet grass,
every rock, and cement gash
in your driveway
on a single walk
from your stoop
to the door of my car;
i should have known then
that a woman should never see the world beneath her
when she leaves the home of a man
who truly loves her.

thank you for never asking to be friends.
because i don't think i actually could be
with a person
who never wondered if i got home safe
the night my heart stumbled off your front lawn
bleeding without bandage
into an endless downpour
of salt.

and when no one was looking
i stole his attention and borrowed his lips
aggressively believing
that's all it would take
to cure a wandering mind
routinely mundane moments
and a list of questions
that somehow constructed itself
inside the small space of existence in this room
that separated his body
and mine.

—ignore the distance

i need to drink
the dawn of that day,
please let me pour myself a nice tall glass;
to swallow the sunbeams that woke these eyes,
woke these eyes from such an innocent rest.
let the morning burn through in its mustard shades,
drip onto my skin and toast to the ways
it whispers in warmth,
"keep rest, darling,"
oh, i need to drink
the dawn of that day.
i need to drink
the dawn of that day
for my lips would not flirt with the rim.
i would throw it back in one big wave,
till the thoughts of you could no longer bear to swim;
let conscience flow free throughout my veins,
impairing my reason for enduring the pain,
strengthening my will to sleep you away,
oh, how i wish i drank
the dawn of that day.

—a redo please

gone are the times i melted your shell.
gone are the times i breathed your bones into existence.
gone are the times that we mattered.
every ounce of carbon was drained from our core,
for you didn't see safe and identifiable in my structure
mostly because i chose to live.
i chose to welcome my composition,
layers deep it may be.
i chose the equivocation of love,
aware of what it could do to my surface daily.
i chose all my vulnerability,
all my faults, and every storm that ever changed me,
knowing that it is within a person's weathering that
you are able to know their story.
i am unafraid of mine,
and i was unafraid of yours.
but you walked.
and while i may have bathed in silence,
my heart need not.
for she is already clean
and standing tall with her last request:
you will take him along with you—
for there is nothing more confusing in this life
than parting ways with a human
and consenting that your souls be left
hand in hand.

one moon,
two sighs,
and an infinity of stars later,
she grabs the side of her pillow,
and listens to the hums of her mind—
like a broken faucet that drips throughout the night.
she could never find peace in silence,
nor ever find peace of mind.
but she never dreamed of the things that made her whole.
she never dreamed of the things that made her still.
she never dreamed of the things people could really understand.
for her dreams were limitless, and in her mind, so was he;
she was a dreamer,
but she did not just dream.
for dreams do end, and to her,
he was someone to live forever.
but somehow during the light hours of a day,
the crowds in her subconscious cheer on the good in him,
showcasing in her mind what she has been missing,
cueing blackouts on faults,
spotlights on fames.
and just as she finds an ounce of strength
to see his act beyond center stage,
curtain drops,
eyes awake,
and time hands her another day.

the first time i held fire,
it didn't just burn.
it danced strangely in my palm,
with a cryptic smile like it knew i was missing out on something vital;
but it was i that adored the definition of such a bold emotion to reap.
it was i that lost sensation staring into my hands of periled pleasure.
it was i that bought the tickets to my show.
and it was i that fell surprised when my life performance had plunged
just as i did.
i played with it, and they told me not to
because my hands were not made of ice—
somehow my detention for breaking this rule wasn't
forty-five minutes staring at a cement wall in grade school,
but rather two years of unrequited love-themed poems,
unexplainable tears that got infamously pinned on hormonal cycles,
callous and unexciting dates to fill these gaps of loneliness,
recycled phrases from family and friends of why i am better off,
and pounds of excuses i ate for breakfast
that fed my incapability to love.
yet i could never be one of those women,
who lies still on a bed with one thousand rose petals floating
sadly toward the floor, pondering
if he loves me or if he loves me not—
for if a question like so ever crosses my mind,
i will then know truth
that he does not.

—consequences of curiosity

i must have sensed some deal breaker,
but i quickly swore that i don't smoke
as if i wasn't one of those girls
to casually inhale heart-racing highs,
hit after hit,
light after light,
chucking vicious laughter toward those
not convinced of my fine composure—
pretending each one would not change me,
down to very depths of nights i wasted
i was still getting wasted, alone.
by dawn, i stood determined to get it right.
but trapped in my trivia, weak in my will,
repeatedly blowing rings of youth into the air,
i somehow hoped they found themselves shoved down
inside the base of your lungs
so for once you can feel what i felt in your presence—
powerless.

he said he wanted to be my moon
so he could light my darkest nights
simply with one revolution around my soul;
but it wasn't until i watched him closely,
bits of him disappeared as my darkness fell—
his phases half hiding,
quarter smiling
at some other world—
i should have known then
oh, silly me,
the moon does not shine for just one girl.

—actions speak louder

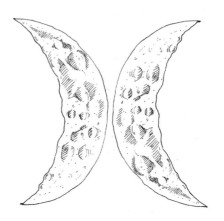

mysterious must be the word
because i have never ran up to a roof
only to dangle my back
and salty hair over some rusted rail
that barely prevented me from flying onto city streets;
hands cushioned their way to the curves on my frame
reminding me of my gender
shushing all hesitations with innocent laughter
promising a phone call the next day
and inching my chin up slowly toward his
protecting and feeling me in a way
that satisfied this desire to be seen in the world.
for he didn't even know my middle name
or how the circled scar once formed above my left eye
but he heard me—
and for once,
that was enough.

as a child, i always dreamed i would fall to love by words spoken,
there i lie in his arms and hear his profession as a fine soliloquy,
one i could entrust dear to my heart like a shiny, gold token,
and his love would form lines oh so poetically.
cinematically filling expectations a young girl rightfully has,
yet speech has evolved.
what a fleeting,
forgotten,
fallow string of words we spit out
to cushion pauses we label as awkward,
filling our minds and draining our hearts with
the overabundance of phrases and suave structure of sentences;
there are no breaks for absorption,
no quivers in our voices,
no stalls for silence,
but our words,
they are a noble choice.
it is sad, and i have heard enough;
i have heard enough to know that ears alone are useless for me to love.
they do not shun the one who courts,
but they cannot aid him either;
for we are no longer a generation to listen,
but one to incessantly speak.
so how can i love by mere words spoken
when words alone have grown so weak?

i recall committing myself to the unknown,
insisting that i would stay forever.
but there was something inside that man that believed
i was the moonlight to drip through his bedroom window;
how i could illuminate his darkened room,
yet what disappointment i brought by day.
and how i had this stream of solace that seemed to fade by dawn.
he knew what kind of bursting love i had.
he smiled like it was enough,
but he carried himself with confusion
for his face and heart were oil and vinegar,
both demanding his demeanor to prove
which held the greater weight upon the two;
i used to blame myself for not being strong enough
to blend his solution,
to lend him peace,
but it was never my concern to be the balance in between;
and so he held such a conviction that he could never love
so tight, so proud inside his hollow chest
that if his heart were to burst and i ripped mine out
to place in his hands,
he still would have felt
that my love was not enough.

i trust you will find someone,
someone fitting for the kind of man that you are,
but i cannot help to feel sad for you
knowing that the one woman who would have placed
the entire world at your feet
was once knocking on your door
and all you ever had to do was open.

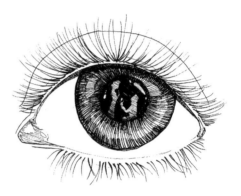

IV

sometimes, i think God saves the heartaches
for all the artists
the musicians
the dancers
and the writers;
for He knows they can touch more lives with their pain
than they ever would if sorrow had not
sailed through their souls.

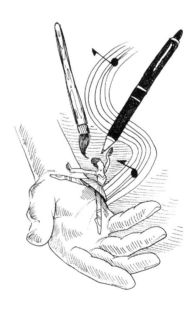

just remember,
through the confusion of life
we were created to be different:
different gifts, different loves,
different pains, different pleasures,
different vices, different virtues,
different paths, different purposes,
but one thing remains the same—
if God led you somewhere,
God will not leave you there.
if you are not moving,
that does not mean that you are not learning.
that does not mean that you are stuck
for when life feels like nothing but a standstill,
God is waiting for our minds to stay still.
something within life right now has been
identified by Him as worthy of attention
and necessary to assist in finding
the abundant peace our hearts incessantly quest for;
yet if resisting His call for our care
is what we choose to do,
we will always find it difficult
to discern what we're going through.

do not ask others to build the house of your success.
you will never know the quality of the
materials, tools, and fabrics
they picked up along the way to help you build your home—
when you control making the choices in your contracting
you gain awareness of the full composition
that constitutes your core foundation.

every so often,
God strips a writer from a coffee shop,
a painter from a canvas,
a pianist from keys,
a speaker from a podium,
and tosses them into a heater of life,
melting and making malleable
the surface they grew too comfortable in—
the surface that became a sole basis for their perception in creating art,
not because He doesn't love us,
but because He loves us so much that we ought to
write,
paint,
play,
sing,
move,
laugh,
love,
listen,
and serve, renewed
with a transformed love so humble, so understanding
that it could soften the saddest of sinners,
silently crying to go back Home.

you cannot ask God
for the armor and weapons to help you win the battle
and also want to be benched on the side the whole time—
for safety is not a servant to strength.

and during the Last Supper
Jesus broke His bread and passed it around the table
towards hands that were too weak to hold Him—
hands that handed Him over
in exchange for money
and Hands that flustered in fury to affirm denial three times;
Jesus did this merely to explain a truth:
no matter the strength or weakness
that resides within our flesh day to day
He chooses us
He forgives us
He heals us
and He wants us
to consume Him.

pain is just pain until we understand how it serves God
then it is no longer pain, but rather
purpose—
for if our pain is deep enough to cast a light up
toward the Kingdom of Heaven,
then so be it—
let us suffer,
if it shines upon the face of our Lord.

no one can put out your fire
when your accelerant is God.

i hope you know it's wiser to pick yourself up
and preach
than to beat yourself up
and weep—
for you cannot be a disciple for God
when you have chosen to bury yourself
beneath.

the beautiful thing about God—
He clears the path of all resistance
when He is ready to make a move in your life.

Your Word feeds my life
like a starving stem sitting
in a potted plant
abandoned by clouds
i have been drained—
but these roots of mine wait
to feel your rain
for i know You,
and i need You, God
day
after
day.

your demons laugh because you've been rejected,
and yet
your angels smile because they know
you are protected.

maybe the point of knowing him wasn't to make him mine.
maybe for the small amount of time
my heart felt like a million sparks set it on fire;
i began to feel again and believe there will be someone out there one day
whom i will fall madly in love with.
his presence gave me a glimpse into the future
and closure from my past.
God is gentle, and He doesn't play with our hearts.
so when He tries to close a door,
He understands why we often put our foot in the way.
we don't believe something so alive could be felt twice in our lifetime,
but that is where we are wrong.
and the way we act in our mere moments of hopelessness
are testaments itself to how much faith we say we have.

do not fret
when you see construction work being done
on the road to your dreams—
for one day, you will sigh peacefully
when it is revealed to you
that the detour was a necessity.

you are the main event
not the opener
so act like you are worth
selling out an arena
and grab the best seats in the house
to enjoy your show—
you are not the option
the fall back plan
the string along for a bit
and see what happens type of person—
so for that alone
do not settle for a life or a love
that fails to act in
seeing and putting
you first.

just remember that when
you bring much to the table
many around you will become enamored
with their options of what is available to be consumed—
but please remember,
you deserve to take the time
to serve yourself too.

date someone who doesn't make you chase them,
but rather wants you to chase God,
and date someone
who wants to chase Him with you.

relationships may find the legs to run
but God grants them the wings to fly.

just so you know
God doesn't have peripheral vision when it comes to us
when everyone and everything that He sees
has always been
within focus.

just remember—
it is never a loss
if God is the gain.

and just when you think you've sprinkled all of yourself to past lovers
in different cities,
different restaurants,
different bedrooms thinking,
this is it,
this is all it can ever be,
God can still pull a fast one on you.
He can gift you the untouched copy of your heart that
He guards in his hands—
the one untainted by this world,
free in its innocence,
and capable of great love;
this heart He will happily give you.
so now you can truly love this one this time—
unafraid,
undamaged,
unconditionally.
you see,
our past can never define who we are capable of becoming,
and what we are capable of feeling
when we have a God that breathes forgiveness.
all we ever have to do is just ask.

—the power of forgiveness

growing up means growing outside
your comfort zone—
not always will it be easy
but always it will be worth it.

"you make me a better person,"
he said to me over and over.
at first i believed it,
smiling and taking credit
for the change in his behavior
and the joy in his life.
but that's not love.
love doesn't plagiarize
what God writes;
for when love knows the author,
it cites the source freely,
holding a mirror up
to show that person the best parts
that were always there
living inside and breathing in them, as a child of God.
he thinks i changed his life,
yet all i ever did was
be the reflection he needed
in a time when he could not see
how his heart beats so beautifully
in this broken world.

i did not think i was strong enough
to fill the shoes God gave me
until He made my feet grow once more
and said to me,

"My child, it is time that you take larger steps in this world."

i didn't always understand the outcome
or why it felt as if life paused on me just as i was beginning to smile.
and yet one day,
i saw my honest reflection,
and the realization became quite clear;
maybe God keeps us on the sidelines
because He knows if we played the game,
we would want to change the rules.

a person finds joy when they truly understand
that it comes from building
a relationship with God
not with man.

it isn't until the very person you love in this world
is fighting for their right to exist
do you understand that prayers become more than a colloquial phrase;
they birth into the last hope that holds our breath
when the final block of life jenga is pulled out beneath us
collapsing our consolation that we scrounge for
in a time to battle whatever verbiage
is about to pierce our ears
upon the presence
of a white coat entering our numbered room
with a confirmed, sullen face and
a syringe to suck out the oxygen
in the air
that we can no longer breathe
either.

he was too young to have a face
pale, painted, and parallel
to fresh flowers
that kindly asked the despair in her soul
to believe that his exit from this world
was just as beautiful as his entrance—
but it wasn't,
and i cannot say who has it worse:
she who wears black and cries at night,
or he who wishes for another day
to bid goodbye.

—too soon

and just when she no longer had to answer to herself
the world dressed itself in a black suit and
threw her into a windowless box of a room
probing questions
over a table, under surveillance
waiting for some break or bead
of sweat to supply
the skeptics and suspicious
with evidential freedom
to defame her new name
with old guilt.

—hardships of becoming someone new

take the clip out of your hair
let the breeze comb it for you
feel the tapping of gentle rain against your skin
and breathe deep—
hear the laughter stream down
past the flowing river
smell the wooden chips that smoked themselves
to travel to the edge of your nose.
you've ran away hoping all this would do you good
maybe you'd forget
and you keep calling upon yourself for something
you keep thinking that you're lacking some passionate love
life has you worried about what you won't be
so much that you are failing to see
how God has specifically chosen your soul to prove to this world that
you are here
you are real
you are alive.

write it

because thoughts become words

words become lines

lines become paragraphs

paragraphs become chapters

chapters become a book

and that book could change someone's life.

so maybe in life it was never about the one
who looked like they had it all on paper
or even the one who paid extensive lip service to see a smile;
sometimes it's about the one true person
who sprinted to all ends of this confusingly wide earth
and collected the shattered pieces of us
that exploded over lands and oceans from the last one.
sometimes it's about the one who repackages and repaints us
with one kiss, one touch,
and tacitly apologizes on behalf of every year they were not there;
for sometimes, it's not about the one
who wants to travel the world with you,
but the one who was traveling through time to love you
before they even knew you.

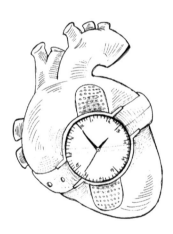

i'd rather have my heart
break because i loved
than feel the ache in regret
that i did not.

i was so busy filling
spaces
pockets
hollow holes of empty
nooks i made
ones i didn't
patching
stitching
piecing
pulling
to make sense of my own sorrows
to question how life could do me wrong
to wonder why clocks still ticked when i couldn't breathe
to ask why i had to drift so far
so far from what i felt
so far from who i was
in the hopes to find who i am;
i was so busy filling
voiding the pain
like it was all a mistake in my life register
and i needed to keep myself contained
limited to what
i only knew myself to be;
i was so busy filling
to string myself along
that i failed to realize how badly breaks are needed
to let this spirit grow
but the mind feels the fear in questioning
the true elasticity of a spirit
and what it can endure;
so out of love
it locks it down

with chains so heavy and keys so small
it becomes no wonder
why no one else can free us
but ourselves.

you are not the nasty words they post online
you are not the books they knock down in the hallway
you are not the weak one shoved in a corner by five troubled souls
you are not the smirks forming or fingers pointing
you are not the snickers in a cafeteria room
you are not the threats they pin against people
you are not what they do.
but you are what you do.
for somehow along the way
they lost touch of what kind of God they have
and isn't it sad that no one told them?
you wake up every morning wondering what the new suffering is going to be
and who is going to hurt you today
but you will not be moved by a spirit on this earth
when you intimately know your God;
acknowledging that scares them because they don't understand Him
they don't understand how you could beat them without weapons
that their eyes can see
or their hands can touch
because one who is truly wise knows the greatest weapons come from within
for they are the only way to fight and guarantee
that they will not be used against you—
your compassion
your kindness
your humility
your leadership
your bravery
your diplomacy
your example
your love
slowly saving your life, the lives of many children
and adults who weren't as bold as you
to believe what you believe

134

because such an understanding
takes a strong person to acknowledge and stand up for the growth in pain
and a very weak person
to cause it.

—anti-bullying

you walk into an empty room
drunken laughter
too much touching
nosy questions
no one listening
and you wonder
why you give in
to the pressure of catching up
when you would never
want to catch up
to them.

—social anxiety

get off the couch and remember
pity is a choice
life doesn't happen to you
and your decisions can make
or break the pieces of you that are still left
it is not romantic to believe you are not in control
it is horrific to think that after all of this
after all the work
we toss up the most important pieces
of our beings in this life
to skate with stars in the sky
and await the universe to mail to us
some formal rejection letter
that explicates why
we are not enough.

fear—
what terrible disease to have
trading in the hope of today
for the distress of tomorrow
stumbling over edits inside this book
overthinking and replacing originality of heart
with conformity and reason.
fear—
what a terrible tyrant to lead us
requiring all to abide by rules
it somehow convinced us
the world had set long ago.

—fear does not exist unless we allow it

ABOUT THE AUTHOR

As a girl, I chose writing to help me understand growth and all the life encounters a young person typically has. As a woman, I no longer chose writing. Writing took over and chose me. Late nights, early mornings, before work, after work, nights out, nights in, wherever, whenever. It became my preferred method of transportation to travel toward a destination of peace. It became the only way I knew to help others embrace their life leaps. Woven into the lines of this book, I speak for those whose hands are empty to hold and hearts that have fallen asleep. Through *Water Lilies*, I debut an exposition of the hurt in humanity, the beauty in boldness, the courage in charity, the raw in recovery, the healing of heart, and the love to exist in the gift of a lifetime.

travel with me—
and take me as i am
believe me when i say
my heart will understand
love with me—
and let us revel in a lovers craze
the girls and boys that make us laugh
on far lesser days
hurt with me—
for the nights i heard words
and placed my heart in hands
that watered down my worth
grieve with me —
and catch my tears that fall
goodbye is something we've all gave
to moments that once stood tall
heal with me—
and smile, because i will for you.
my heart has stretched its limits
but i know that
yours has too.

Printed in the United States
By Bookmasters